About the Author

Houda Younes is a Lebanese writer and educator. After completing her bachelor's degree in Biology and a Master's degree in Food Science at the University of Balamand, she became a biology and chemistry educator. Currently, she is pursuing another Master's degree in Clinical Psychology at the University of Social Sciences and Humanities in Warsaw.

Implementing her scientific background in students' academic life was very enjoyable, but guiding them through their teenage years was her foremost delight. As she delved into their dreams and ambitions, they ignited an old flame of one of her dearest passions in life. She started writing and editing science school books and manuals, but above all that, she dived back into the beautiful world of poetry. Her poems fostered her childhood's imagination, her adolescent struggles, and her adulthood's reflections on life. Houda believes that poetry is a therapeutic sanctuary for the sorrows and joys of memorable moments that unite people.

Dedication

To my first and everlasting love, my family:
Salwa, Fawzi, Yara, Farah, Majd, Roula, and Lynn;

To my precious Godmother Nawal;

To every struggling teenager;

To every lost soul searching for hope, love, and beauty in life;

To the little dreamer inside of me and inside of every one of us;

I dedicate this book to you.

Dream, believe, and you will achieve.

Houda Younes

RHYMES OF LIFE AND LOVE

AUSTIN MACAULEY PUBLISHERS™
LONDON • CAMBRIDGE • NEW YORK • SHARJAH

Copyright © Houda Younes 2022

The right of Houda Younes to be identified as author of this work has been asserted in accordance with section 77 and 78 of the Copyright, Designs and Patents Act 1988.

All rights reserved. No part of this publication may be reproduced, stored in a retrieval system, or transmitted in any form or by any means, electronic, mechanical, photocopying, recording, or otherwise, without the prior permission of the publishers.

Any person who commits any unauthorized act in relation to this publication may be liable to criminal prosecution and civil claims for damages.

A CIP catalogue record for this title is available from the British Library.

ISBN 9781398402706 (Paperback)
ISBN 9781398402713 (ePub e-book)

www.austinmacauley.com

First Published 2022
Austin Macauley Publishers Ltd
1 Canada Square
Canary Wharf
London
E14 5AA

Acknowledgements

I extend my gratitude and appreciation to:

my amazing cousin and life-long friend, Zeina, for designing a beautiful book cover;

my lovely ladies, Samantha, Cendrella, and Simona for their endless love and inspiration;

my dear friends, Christelle, Celine, Eliz, and Roudy, for their joyful brainstorming and endless encouragement;

to Austin Macauley Publishers for believing in my talent and providing me with a great professional opportunity to publish my collection of poems.

I thank you all for your support and confidence in my work.

Poems

Section One: Rhymes of Life 11

    Bird with No Feathers 12

    Life in Moments 14

    Five Minutes 16

    Sailors of Life 18

    Breathe 19

    Let It Rain 20

    Detach 21

    Embrace the Unknown 22

    Look Up 23

    Good Things Take Time 24

    Destination 25

    Dare to Be You 26

    Close Your Eyes 27

    She Was Asleep 28

    Deep Within 29

    In the Darkness 30

    Lovely Angel 31

    Into the Blue 32

    Between the Winds 33

    Restless Soul 34

    Falling Leaves 35

    Loved Ones 36

    Identity 37

    Tomorrow Is Near 38

    Echoing Laughter 39

    To Hell... No, to Heaven 40

Section Two: Rhymes of Love 43

    Glorious Eyes 44

    Love 45

    The One 46

Love in Roses	47
Missing the Memories	48
Those Nice Days	49
Thank You	50
Pounding in My Heart	52
Missing Him	53
Gossip and Love	54
You Were a Dream	55
Like No One Will	56
The Silver Phone	57
Rewind	58
Dancing Words	59
Tears of Love	60
A Story of Love	61
What Happened?	62
Who Is She?	64
Broken Rose	65
Why?	66

SECTION ONE: RHYMES OF LIFE

Bird with No Feathers

First, you are born, then you open your eyes
With your mind so empty and yet so clear
No one knowing if you're stupid or wise
Only knowing how cute you are and dear.

Your heart feels your nice mother
Who held you for long nights and days
Who taught you how to love her
In her unique passionate ways.

Then comes your lovely dad
Who works for you day and night
To never see you sad
And keep your life shining bright.

You grow up…

Suddenly, without knowing how
All your parents' fear
Will be suffocating you now
With words you can't hear.

Now all you want to be is like others
Go out with girls and boys, friends of your age.
You don't know you're a bird with no feathers
In its most significant vulnerable stage.

Your parents try to protect you
By always saying "no"
They're only doing what they do
Based on what they know.

You cannot blame them, they cannot let go…
They were young just like you, a long time ago
And they forgot that wings by themselves grow
And young feathers can fall off from one blow.

Then you indulge in your own mistakes
You trust, you doubt, you win, you lose, you love and you hate
The more you give life, the more it takes
The more you live it, the closer you get to your fate.

Then you find out that your wings grew
And your feathers got stronger
Now you know better what to do
And you can't wait any longer.

You can now see your mother's love and your father's
You remember your nice, pure innocence
Which was lost by every blow on your feathers
Always trying to ruin your happiness.

Now you are older and you're more cautious
You know that life is an ongoing complicated fight
Now you know what deserves to be precious
And what deserves your little innocent tears at night.

Yet, this is not the end
It will never actually stop
You'll never comprehend
How your wings and feathers grow up.

You can always be a bird
With feathery wings
That flies all around the world
And happily sings.

Yet the song may make you cry
And the feathers can fall any day
So, if this day you can't fly
Fight, don't give up, and don't run away!

Life in Moments

Three, two, one... say cheese!
Hold on to beauties and keep your smile
Hold on to this breeze
Linger in that moment for a while.

C'est la vie!

The essence of all happiness
Life of glee!
Shining through moments of greatness.

Appreciate every long walk
Appreciate every short run
Enjoy every sweet little talk
Enjoy hugs that set with the sun.

Enjoy the glow of green eyes
Enjoy every step by the sea
Listen to truths behind lies
Watch the darkness before you see.

Listen to the tone of every voice
Listen to the sound of the leaves
Rustling in the calm wind to rejoice
The eternal return of beliefs.

Bend your knee to walk over the sand
To feel its tenderness all over your little toes
Bend your arm to hold on to a hand
To keep it close to your heart so that it never goes.

Laugh happily from deep down
Every time you feel it
Move away every bad frown
Every time you face it.

Live each moment of your day
Not all exquisite moments can be repeated
Live to stay here when away
The glory of life can never be defeated.

Five Minutes

It takes five minutes only
to call an old friend
to drink a nice beer
for scars to amend.

It takes five minutes only
to kiss your nice wife
to hold your kids
for a blissful life.

It takes five minutes only
to read resourceful lines
to memorise a special quote
for wisdom that shines.

It takes five minutes only
to pick what to dine
to enjoy your meal
with a sip of wine.

It takes five minutes only
to argue for the defence
to stand out for your rights
with no grudge and no offense.

It takes five minutes only
to say a steady, strong no
to refuse what you hate
without going with the flow.

It takes five minutes only
to help a grandma cross the wide street
to buy a poor homeless man some good food
without asking if he wants to eat.

It takes five minutes only…

to see the world as your big plan
to plant precious hope for your homeland
to uphold justice when you can
to take initiative from where you stand.

It takes five minutes only…

Sailors of Life

We are just sailors
Boarding the waves of life
Challenging failures
Avoiding useless strife.

Sailors we are every day
Passing through countless gusty storms
That will either lead us astray
Or build us essential reforms.

When on deck, we let down every sail
For wind to blow our ship in one direction
Yet we steer the rudder down to scale
And decide on every changing deflection.

Breathe

Breathe in all your sorrows
and let them out as hope
wishing that what follows
brings you the strength to cope.

Breathe in all your inner fears
and let them out as a quest
which lets the broken cohere
freeing but only your best.

Breathe in your lost and failing steps
and let them out as a success
reformulating their concepts
away from all misery and stress.

Let It Rain

Nice leaves are falling
Friend after a friend
Nature is calling
For a season's end.

Let lightning crack your heart
Let the rain wash away your fear
Let this end be a new start
Let the raging thunder go clear.

Listen to the waterdrops
Knocking on your window glass
A rhythm that never stops
Leading all your pain to pass.

Let it rain with all joy
And let the water flow by
To let your eyes enjoy
Rising rainbows in the sky.

Detach

Risk it, it is worth it!
Let go… detach and leave!
Believe in your power
and what you will achieve.

Do not be afraid
to break out of your shell
and grab those voices
back to heaven from hell.

Shatter the haunting loud shouts
coming from those who do not know
who criticise just to… be
enjoying their high when you're low.

You make your identity
you are what you choose
if you fail, fall and get up
then you'll never lose.

Embrace the Unknown

Seems it's true
Embrace infinities with the unknown
Fear no blue
Because your smile will flourish on its own.

The road is so long
You will always have to stand up
Have faith to be strong
Never say no, never give up.

God has prepared a bigger plan
So let Him lead the way
All insightful stories began
When He gave hope to stay.

Look Up

Keep Smiling
Reach Out.
Stop Nagging.
Hang out.

Life is unfair.
But it's joyful.
Live to declare
What is hopeful.

The sky is your limit.
Keep on looking up.
Live every minute.
Learn to develop.

Good Things Take Time

It takes twenty-four hours
To give birth to a new day
It takes years to build towers
That glow from far, far away

It takes thirty days for our moon
To rise in the dark fully bright
It takes long nights to invent a tune
That will spread a joyful delight.

It takes nine months to give life
For whom happiness is prime
Let go of worries and strife
Because all the good things take time.

Destination

Everyone wants it.
Few have the courage to live it.
Few take risks for it.
And many just dream of it.

It is not hard to be free.
Just believe and commit.
Choose wisely your referee.
Persevere and don't quit.

Go and travel alone.
Go on a vacation.
Explore the unknown.
Find your destination.

Get lost to find yourself.
Fail so that you succeed.
Expand your young bookshelf.
You'll be free when you read.

Dare to Be You

Dare to be different
Dare to be true
Dare to be aspirant
Dare to be you!

If you never give up on your dream
It will never give up on you.
Know that every day, the sunrays beam
Inspiring what you should do.

Dare to fall and fail
And afterward, dare to rise
Persist to prevail
By teaching how to be wise.

Expect to lose many friends
On your pathway to succeed.
When a relationship ends
Another one will proceed.

Dare to see the truth inside
Hidden beneath lost souls
Scattered in their life behind
Their superficial roles.

Close Your Eyes

Close your eyes.
Don't just blink.
Close your eyes.
Try to think.

Are you really joyful?
Are you truly self-satisfied?
Are you strong and hopeful
to face it all and never hide?

Does your smile come from your heart
or you just do it to pretend
that today is a new start
and you do not want it to end?

Set your goal.
Try to think.
Touch your soul
with every blink.

She Was Asleep

She was constantly asleep
before the alarm rang
pulling her from the deep
where she had used to hang.

She passionately woke up
from her dying fake dreams
to eagerly halt and stop
all those social mainstreams.

She was afraid of adventure
she surrendered to all the norms
now she is ready to venture
to lead her aspired reforms.

Deep Within

We go through life
Not knowing where to go
We get lost on roads
We barely even know.

We seek redemption
For every sad and angry night
But we always forget
Healing is never black and white.

We try to run away from sorrows
And hide between our injury cracks
We forget that strength is inside us
But fear is covering its guiding tracks.

We love to see the sunrise
And believe in its bright light
But we forget that to reach its glow
Darkness is what we'll have to fight.

We want the positivity
Yet we give up and cry
We forget that only after those tears
We rise from the ashes – up so high.

We all have endless questions
And we search for answers in every virtue and sin
But we forget that the only answer we need
Comes from a peaceful place deep down within.

In the Darkness

Beware of complete closure
Always open up
Not for complete exposure
Nor for a close-up.

Speak to a friend
A trustworthy one
Don't reach the end
When you've just begun.

Don't be ashamed
To ask for all help
You won't be blamed
For a life's misstep.

Your thoughts matter
Your healthy psyche does too
You'll get better
Many are there for you!

Do not worry about the darkness
Overwhelming your life in this fight
Gather up your courageous wellness
To pass out of that tunnel into the light.

Lovely Angel

Come, lovely angel, and take me away
Come take away my fears
Come, lead me back to the righteous way
Come wipe away my tears.

Come relieve my pain
Come let me free
Come vanquish my strain
Come let me be…

Send me a nice smile from you
Send me a joyful loyal friend
Send me love, one that's true
Send me insight to comprehend.

Send me a great relief
Send me happiness
Send me a strong belief
Send me forgiveness.

Into the Blue

When I am angry at the whole wide world
I just rush into you
When nothing can explain it, not a word
I dive into the blue.

When I'm lost in a flow
Of dashing thoughts and pain
Into your deeps I go
To dissolve this stressful strain.

Over there, it's a different way…
Over there, I'm boundless and free
I can for ever and ever stay
Swimming in the waves of the sea.

The sense of the refreshed oceans
Brings out the inner light inside me
And transforms my true devotions
To swimming and swirling in the sea.

It is my world out there
Facing the truth and losing the fear
I won't go anywhere
If I can always only be here.

When I want to express
When I want to be true
When I want to confess
I dive into the blue.

It's the heart of peace and joy
It's pure beauty with a pretty shine
One will pleasantly enjoy
How heavenly it is and divine.

Between the Winds

Here I sit between the winds
Just feeling the sweet fresh air
Here I sit between the winds
While no one is ever there…

Am I really alone
Or just gone blind?
Are there plenty around
Whom I can't find?

Is it true we can't know
What's life about, this mystery
Or is it just right there
But we are too blind to see?

We never know what we have
Until we lose it for too long
Then regret consumes our soul
And we become both weak and strong.

We never are satisfied
Because life can always give
We get mad, then sad and hurt
And we forget to forgive.

There I sit between the winds
Taking in a breath of fresh sweet air
There I sit between the winds
Wondering if someone will be there…

Restless Soul

Dreams and hopes just fly around
In the endless sleepless nights
Hoping for peace to be found
Away from all harmful fights.

All the day thinking
And analysing it all
The self forgetting
Torturing the restless soul.

Exhausted from the long patience
For a lost unknown
Sick and tired of the stiffness
When standing alone.

Dreams and hope just fly around
Eager to know what to do
Searching for a common ground
To venture out of their blue.

Falling Leaves

The storm suddenly blew
My blossomed roses withered
My heart went into a blue
My lingering smile shivered.

When opening a heart's vein
Lonely chirping birds fled away
Leaving love, patience and pain
To grow each and every day.

The beautiful blowing breeze
Is now blowing sadness and tears
Shutting open doors of lost keys
Silencing joyful happy cheers.

It was all summer and spring
Flourishing happily all the way
With tremendous joy to bring
Then winter came to darken the day.

All the birds still fly
As well as the nice swans and geese
Blue will still be the sky
Yet nothing stops the falling leaves.

Loved Ones

I can bear between us blue seas
Life in deep, dark valleys with revolting, rusty air
I can bear the permanent buzz of the bees
But the thought of losing you, that I cannot bear.

Listening to depressing people all day
Lost in their vague ideas and whirled
Is extremely easy if with me you will stay
Together, we will beautify the world.

I will welcome death if it comes near
Just not near any one of you
It is my oldest deepest fear
For I shall be lost without you.

Identity

If only I can free the hurt and pain
Out to nowhere till they disappear
Will I have anything at all to gain
Because nothing is actually clear?

Innocent hearts are gone
Trust is fading away
Tell me what could be done
To not go astray.

This is the normal trend anyway
This is how people are acting
If you are not with them in that bay
Then you're practically not living.

Then, am I the one dead?
Or am I the one alive
And they're dead instead
Trying on lies to strive?

Tomorrow Is Near

Tomorrow is a few hours away
Yet the dawn of enlightenment seems so far
Many generations are led astray
Humanity fading like a dying star.

I wish you love yourselves
Through loving others
I wish you books on shelves
To wake your brothers.

I wish you loads of compassion
For all of the worldwide spread injustice
I wish you inspired passion
Yearning for highly ambitious fairness.

I wish you all the love and patience
To listen to those unprivileged in need
To open your hearts with clearance
Away from all of the devastating greed.

Tomorrow is a few hours away
Try to make it be an unforgettable steer
Be the change you want to be now, today
For today is tomorrow… but a bit near.

Echoing Laughter

At the end of every day
At the beginning of every night
Nothing will forever stay
But memories in every twilight…

Memories of echoing laughter
And of joyful shouts
Memories of forever after
And of sweet hangouts.

To Hell... No, to Heaven

How many times
Have you said it?
It's not so wise
To express it.

"To hell with it,"
You say and go
"Enough of it
I will let go."

It's good you are shouting out loud
You're rejecting your situation
But it's not your voice, it's a sound
Of mere negative exhalation.

Yes. It is true.
"To hell" let it be
But continue
"To heaven with me".

Shout, get mad and angry but don't wait.
Instead, you must learn what to do:
That is to love and appreciate
Only one single person: YOU!

Don't criticise and get sad
Criticise to change and achieve
Criticise to move ahead
And if you can't, then simply leave.

To hell with being down
To heaven with rising up
Wear that elegant gown
Walk through your dream and don't stop!

SECTION TWO: RHYMES OF LOVE

Glorious Eyes

Wondering in this beautiful wide world
Trying to figure out *me* between all the *I*'s
Losing myself over the wrong words
Till faith and hope shined in his glorious eyes.

Life, far from being complete,
Was yearning for a long glowing glee
He made her passionate heart beat
resuscitating every systole and diastole.

Shivering between the right and wrong
Day and night, thinking of what to do
Had never been so weak and so strong
Had never been lost in the shades of hue.

When his eyes met her eyes
She knew that he was her calling
She never felt such strong ties
Freeing her from her fear of falling.

Life blossoms through thine embrace
Perfection is near, though it's far away.
Thy smooth kiss brightens my face
Wishing forever with thee I can stay.

Through thy glorious eyes, the stars shine
And for your smile, they twinkle
Just like age glamourizes wine
I hope we grow to wrinkle.

The galaxies won't hold my heart
Because you need more space to dance
You've enchanted me since the start
From that first touch to that first glance.

Love

Love is an option
or is it a must?
Love is adoption
of a soulful lust.

Love is a freedom
glowing in thine eyes
away from boredom
thy sweet heart lies.

Love is contagious
from deep within to thee.
Oh, how invasive
it could forever be.

Love lingers in thy beat
along with every single touch
a bit harsh, a bit sweet
a bit over and a bit too much.

The One

You might be the one…

The one I want to sing songs with
Even though I have a terrible voice
The one I want to get lost with
Even though you are not my only choice.

The one I want to kiss and hug
Every single time we meet
The one I want to draw a smile for
With every single heartbeat.

The one I want to get bored with
When I have nothing at all to do
The one whom I want to laugh with
Even when I'm feeling blue.

The one who always holds my hand
Even when words make me cry
The one who keeps it down to earth
While holding me up so high.

Love in Roses

I thought love was in roses
Simply pink, white and red
In few "I Love You" doses
With fairy tales ahead.

Turns out that it is not
And it is way much more
It could be cold or hot
Once you open that door.

Beauty lies in its fight
To feel, to listen, to endure
To see no black and white
To believe in what's really pure.

Love is to peacefully lose all your hate
Not through a rose or a lingering kiss
But through learning how to appreciate
That happy moments are glamorous bliss.

Missing the Memories

It's not the person you miss
It's the way he made you feel
It is that hug or that kiss
Exceptionally surreal.

It's those memories which draw smiles
Upon your faces on darkest days
It's that magic holding up for miles
Through these special phenomenal days.

Love shall glow in the light
And no darkness it shall see
With warm passionate insight
Away from hate it shall be.

It's not that person whom you miss
Or that song, that year or day
It's that special moment of bliss
That won't ever fade away.

Those Nice Days

Those nice days no one can deny
Will always linger in my sky.

From the honest smile
While holding my hand
To the flying dreams
With nowhere to land

To the innocent kiss
Of losing control
And to the happy bliss
Of that knocking door.

To the thrilling butterflies
Each time you are near
And the endless happiness
Away from all fear.

Thank You

Thank you for being considerate
Thank you for being so caring
Thank you for being so passionate
Thank you for being so loving.

Thank you for being the joy
I had been searching for for years
Thank you for being the boy
Who made me embrace all my fears.

Thank you for being the caring man
Who enlightened the shy woman in me.
Thank your for being my number one fan
In whatever I was, am, or decide to be.

Thank you for picking me up at any stop
And keeping me close and warm
Thank you for never allowing me to drop
Shielding me from any storm.

Thank you for trying to be you
Without affecting me being free
Thank you for the things you would do
To make sure our dreams would one day be.

Thank you for the love you gave me
Thank you for all the laughs and the fun
Thank you for the way you left me
When everything was over, all done.

Thank you for being my lover
Thank you for being my friend
Thank you for being my brother
Standing by me till the end.

Thank for the splendid smiles
Thank you for the wasteful cries
Thank you for the butterflies
A feeling that never dies.

Thank you for all the harsh words at night
Thank you for being a scared child
For whom I always wanted to fight
When all he knew was how to hide.

Thank you for everything, good and bad
Thank you for opening my eyes to see
Thank you for breaking the wings I have had
But mostly, I thank you for changing me!

Pounding in My Heart

Can you see the glow in my eyes
When I daydream of me and you?
Seeing you looking very nice
Leaves me wondering what to do.

I never saw you that way
Very beautiful, magical and true
Am I wanting you to stay
Or am I falling back in love with you?

She suddenly came
To wake me up
To light up an old flame
To burn me non-stop.

Look at me
Just look for once and keep looking
Can't you see
How deep down I am sinking?

I knew you from a start
That's heading to its end
You're pounding in my heart
Not knowing where to stand.

Missing Him

I miss that nice boy
Who adored me once upon a long time
Who filled me with joy
And made my words flow with pretty rhyme.

I miss that boy who used to respect me
Who used to smile with his voice
Who knew what he really wanted to be
Who made me his only choice…

Where and why he didn't say
I did not, do not and will not know
Why that boy had gone away
Leaving raging storms behind to blow.

Gossip and Love

Tell me the truth now
I'm so tired of you
Tell me the truth now
Once in your life, be true.

You go very far away
Leaving me alone for so long
Then you are back for a day
And expect me to be so strong?

Haven't you grown up?
Why can't you make up your mind?
It's now time to stop
And search for a truth to find.

You need to stop asking around
If you want something, come to me
Or else nothing true will be found
Besides gossip and blasphemy.

You Were a Dream

Will you just hold me
So close and tight?
I want you near me
All through the night.

I need to know that this is all true
I need to know that I'm not going to be shocked
I need to know that it's safe to love you
And to open my heart that for long has been locked.

I guess I dreamt a lot
Always trying to shape you in my own way
Into something you're not
Into an image that you cannot convey.

You might be very busy
Well, I am too
But this did not stop me
From calling you.

It won't hurt to ask
Or just say hello
It's not a hard task
But you wouldn't know.

I guess you were my dream
Of hope in love just once again
But you're not what you seem
We ended before we began.

Like No One Will

How come it's never over with me?
I wish you can tell me why.
I cannot see things the way you see.
I'm lost in your gloomy sky.

I told you many times it will not last
But you kept pushing till I surfed with you
We swam through high and low waves in the past
But look at us today… nothing is true.

I'm moving away and wishing you well
So, sweetheart, you can lighten up and chill.
And try not to forget that you once fell
For a girl who loved you as no one will.

The Silver Phone

There it lies in front of me
A silver metallic phone
As near and far it can be
Just sitting there, all alone.

Each time I try to call
Dignity stands in the way
Preventing a new fall
By just keeping you away.

It's time for setting limits, it's true.
It's time for gathering all the strength found.
It's time to stop feeling down and blue
It's time to step on the actual ground.

Logically, that's how it has to be.
That is how our life goes.
You can never hide out or simply flee.
That is how the river flows.

Yet why does logic have to control us
To leave our painful hearts
To leave our feelings in a big fuss
To leave us searching for new starts?

It is very painful, that is known
And all we do is hiding our pain
Pretending we're happily grown
With nothing whatsoever to explain.

There it lies but I can't reach it
To explain how much I miss you and love you
Still, when sometimes I do reach it
I call and start lying to you…

Rewind

Do I ever cross your mind
as often as you cross mine?
Does our story rewind
over a nice glass of wine?

Do you recall those days
when we were happily innocent and young
enjoying sunshine rays
while sharing a revolutionary song?

Do you remember our hopes
that we had never given up on
and all those slippery slopes
that we shouldn't have fallen upon?

Dancing Words

All I have left for you is words
Dancing on lonely lost pages
To a song of our different worlds
Yearning to peacefully meet for ages.

Here, I can endlessly talk
Here, I can infinitely feel
Here, I can aimlessly walk
To a joyfulness so surreal.

Here, I will love you with full rights
With no ethical agreements to foresee.
Here, I will face no fears and fights
For letting my passion rise and be…

Tears of Love

Are you the one who drove me agonised to here?
To here, to this forbidden, dreary earth
Where there will always be an endless constant fear
Where there is nothing, actually, of worth?

As harshly stolid I had ever been
As true happiness has been my truth to seek
Not I who'll trip defeated through a grin
But I who'll rise with the innocence of the meek.

For life shall never stop for yesterday
To thrive on tortured, sorrowed, injured love
But life shall blossom roses day by day
And chant with one successful lovely dove.

A Story of Love

I thought the hardest thing would be letting go
I thought the hardest thing would be forgetting
I thought the hardest thing would be saying no
I thought the hardest thing would be leaving.

I thought we should move away
I thought we should stay apart
I thought we should never stay
I thought I should hush my heart.

Now convinced... I did all this
And surprisingly, moved on
Expecting some kind of bliss
But finally, finding none.

I found a universal truth, it seems
A story of vanishing innocence
Of eternal love and all of its dreams
Of what really lies behind happiness.

A story in which love
Generally gives a bliss as it glows
A story of how love
Selfishly takes it all back as it goes.

A story in which hearts
Unite as an inseparable one
A story of how hearts
Will separate forever to be gone.

What Happened?

They met through typed words on a screen
She enjoyed their long talks each night
And embraced the words she had seen
Twinkling through her computer's light.

As the days passed, her smile grew
And along with it grew her heart
She was feeling something new
Something fresh like a brand-new start.

Then this magical day came
When they knew they loved each other
No other day was the same
Since they became close together.

Then bad days came, fought over and won
So the love story ended here
Yet they still talked together, laughed and had fun
Never feeling far, always near.

Then they started to endlessly fight
Day and night, night and day
Darkness overwhelmed their shining light
Till they faded away.

Her lover, brother, friend and son
Was simply getting out of hand
She tried everything that could be done
Until she could no more pretend.

He's not himself; he's not the same
He shouts, he screams and he gets mad
He turned into a beast to tame
And that made her much more than sad.

What happened? She hated to see him this way
What happened? She hated how he behaved
What happened? Why was he going away?
What happened? Why couldn't he see how he changed?

Who Is She?

What have I done to thee?
Thy smile tender
A long-lost memory.

What have I done to thee?
A long-lost affection
Always runs away to flee.

What have I done to thee?
I've seized the whole world
Devoid of rejoiced glee.

What have I done to thee?
I see happiness
But none of this is free.

What have I done to thee?
Did thee lose thy soul?
Tell me now, who art thee?

Broken Rose

The lightning will strike
From the deepest depth of thine eyes
And the rain shall pour
Upon revealing thy disguise.

Thy soul shall hide
When I just look at thee
Searching for thy pride
Thy words will fly and flee.

Thy heart will go shiver
By thy broken rose
As thy petals wither
For what thou chose.

Why?

Why does it hurt so much?
Why does it wake us up all night?
Why do we miss their touch?
Why do we really have to fight?

Why is the heart broken
If they're in it night and day?
Why leave words unspoken?
Why lead us to go astray?

Was actually loving them that wrong?
Was it worth making us cry?
Loving you them was that confusing song
of a raging hopeless "Why?"

CPSIA information can be obtained
at www.ICGtesting.com
Printed in the USA
LVHW080759030122
707668LV00011B/300